IMAGES
of America

MARYLAND
STEEPLECHASING

Maryland Hunt Cup

Centennial
1894-1994

Saturday, April 30, 1994
4:00 p.m.

In 1994, the Maryland Hunt Cup celebrated its 100th anniversary. The commemorative program featured the Maryland Hunt Cup logo with steeplechase riders flanking the silver tankard.

On the Cover: Riders in the 1968 Grand National create a bucolic portrait galloping across the course. (Courtesy of Peter Winants.)

IMAGES

of America

MARYLAND
STEEPLECHASING

Christianna McCausland

Published by Arcadia Publishing
Charleston SC, Chicago IL, Portsmouth NH, San Francisco CA

Printed in the United States of America

Library of Congress Catalog Card Number: 2005930795

For all general information contact Arcadia Publishing at:
Telephone 843-853-2070
Fax 843-853-0044
E-mail sales@arcadiapublishing.com
For customer service and orders:
Toll-Free 1-888-313-2665

Visit us on the internet at http://www.arcadiapublishing.com

Spectators at the 1970 running of the Maryland Hunt Cup are shown here. (Courtesy of Peter Winants.)

CONTENTS

Acknowledgments   6

Introduction   7

1. Conversation to Competition   9

2. The Thrill of Competition   33

3. The Culture of the Horse   83

4. Yesterday and Today   113

ACKNOWLEDGMENTS

This book would not be possible without the generous contributions of time, support, knowledge, or photography made by the following: Peter Winants, Douglas Lees, Richard and Bert Morgan, Turney McKnight, Rosalie Fenwick, Charles Fenwick Sr., Charles C. Fenwick III, The Maryland Horse Breeders Association, Michael Ewing, Joe G. Davies, the staff of the Enoch Pratt Free Library, *The Maryland Horse* archive, and the many individuals who allowed me into their homes to share their photographs and stories. The following books were also instrumental in putting together this history: *Steeplechasing: A Complete History of the Sport in North America* (2000) by Peter Winants; *Redmond C. Stewart, Foxhunter and Gentleman of Maryland* by Gordan Grand; *The Maryland Hunt Cup Past and Present* (1975) by John Rossell; *The Grand National Steeplechase 1898–1998* (1998) by Margaret Worrall; and *The Will to Win* (1966) by Jane McIlvaine.

Jerry Trone and Kevin Gowl escort Swayo in the paddock of the Maryland Hunt Cup, a race the horse won twice. (Courtesy of Douglas Lees)

INTRODUCTION

Northern Baltimore County at the end of the 19th century was an area of rolling countryside full of dairy and horse farms. Although Baltimore is only a short half-hour drive away now, at that time the rumble of urban life would have been a different world. One of the more popular pursuits for farmers and horse owners at the time—and it remains so today—was fox hunting. In the age-old sport of fox hunting, riders on horseback would gather for a meet and, under the leadership of the huntsman and field master, would follow a pack of hounds out into the wide-open farms and forests of the county to chase foxes. To keep up with the hounds, riders and horses would spend hours galloping over open fields and through woods, jumping over anything that got in their way from stone walls to post-and-rail fences. Fox hunting remains a fast-paced sport that is not for the faint of heart.

The first steeplechase race reportedly took place in 1752 in Ireland, when two friends made a wager to race across country from one church to another in a literal steeple chase. In Maryland, the first recognized steeplechase race was run at Pimlico in the city of Baltimore on October 18, 1873. But it was in the surrounding counties of Baltimore, Harford, and Howard that the sport took hold as competition brewed between hunt clubs.

In 1894, five gentlemen—Frank Baldwin, Henry Farber, Gerard Hopkins, Jacob Ulman, and Ross Whistler—were discussing who among them had the best horse for fox hunting. As the conversation became heated, a challenge was issued: the argument could only be settled with a race. Members of two area hunt clubs, The Elkridge Fox Hunting Club (now the Elkridge-Harford Hunt) and the Green Spring Valley Hunt gathered on May 26, 1894, near Stevenson's Station (currently near the site of St. Paul's School). Twelve horses entered that race; three withdrew, and nine ran the course. Johnny Miller, ridden by his owner, John McHenry, won. The race was so popular it became an annual event.

In 1898, several young men who wanted to compete in the Maryland Hunt Cup but were too young founded a shorter race in which all but one competitor rode ponies. They called it the Grand National, selecting the same name of the renowned steeplechase held in Aintree, England. As the boys grew older, the age limit of 16 was raised, and the race became for horses.

In 1902, the My Lady's Manor race was established, again to settle a dispute over who had the fastest jumper on the Manor (an area of land that was one of the first land grants given by Lord Baltimore). The My Lady's Manor took a short hiatus, becoming an annual event in 1909. Thus the Big Three of Maryland steeplechase racing—the My Lady's Manor, the Grand National, and the Maryland Hunt Club—began.

Each race is founded on the basic principles of fox hunting. The grueling courses, each unique in its terrain and jump configuration, cover between three and four miles of farmland broken by timber jumps (post and rail fences or board), some rising up out of the verdant pasture land to almost five feet high.

Each race changed locations in the early years before establishing their permanent homes: The My Lady's Manor adjacent to the Ladew Topiary Gardens and the Elkridge-Harford

Hunt Club; the Grand National in Butler, Maryland; and The Maryland Hunt Cup in the Worthington Valley. The race season begins with the Elkridge-Harford Hunt races (a great proving ground for young horses and riders that began over 50 years ago) on the first Saturday in April, and continues with the National Steeplechase Association-sanctioned My Lady's Manor, Grand National, and Maryland Hunt Cup, run on the last three consecutive Saturdays of April each year. Only during World War II did the racecourses remain silent in the spring.

As it was in the beginning, the races are open to amateur riders only, and it is not uncommon for a rider to be an owner as well. Each race is a vital stepping-stone to the next. Horses that perform well on the Manor or at the Grand National are likely to go on to the Maryland Hunt Cup, which is still recognized as one of the most esteemed and difficult steeplechase races in the country and the world. As one rider explained, "there is no dress rehearsal for the Maryland Hunt Cup." Over the years, the races have turned horses into hometown heroes, their names ringing through history like warriors of old: Billy Barton, Jay Trump, Mountain Dew, Ben Nevis II, and Pine Pep.

While the races remain enduring symbols of the power of tradition, regardless of war or modern-day suburban sprawl, over the last century, some things have changed. Most notably, women were added to the field of jockeys after Kathy Kushner sued to obtain a Maryland jockey's license in 1968.

In addition to the competition on the field, there are many social traditions that mark the racing season. Even as the fences get higher and more demanding with each race, so the tailgating becomes ever more elaborate too, beginning with picnic hampers at the My Lady's Manor and ending with tailgate spreads that include silver candelabras, linen tablecloths, and over-the-top flower arrangements at the Maryland Hunt Cup. The night of the Maryland Hunt Cup is always the night of the Hunt Ball, one of the last white-tie-and-tail events surviving in Baltimore today. The crowd of spectators grows each year, as more and more urban and suburban families become enthralled with the fast-paced sport of steeplechase racing and the fun alfresco party atmosphere of the day.

An early cameraman gets up-close to the action in a Big Three race from the 1920s.

One

CONVERSATION TO COMPETITION

Though it was wet under foot, May 26 dawned beautiful overhead, and everyone within striking distance of Stevenson Station turned out in carriages, on foot, or on horseback, until it was almost impossible to move on the roads.

—From *The Story of the Maryland Hunt Cup*, published in a 1931 race day program

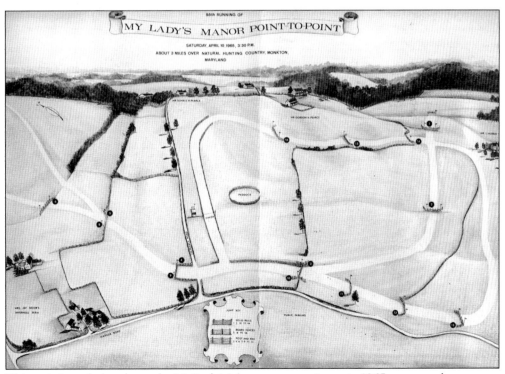

This artist's rendering shows the My Lady's Manor course as it was in 1965, run over the property of the Secor, Pearce, Riggs, and Warfield families in Monkton.

The Elkridge Harford Hunt meet creates a traffic jam in Monkton. Members of the Elkridge Harford Hunt challenged members of the nearby Green Spring Valley Hunt Club to a race in 1894 to determine who had the best horse for hunting, thus initiating the first Maryland Hunt Cup. (Courtesy of Tom Voss.)

A large field from The Green Spring Valley Hunt Club moves off from St. Johns Church in Butler sometime in the 1920s or 1930s led by Frank Dare. The scene has changed little from the time when the Elkridge Harford Hunt's challenge to race was accepted in 1894. (Courtesy of Frank Bonsal.)

Fox hunting remains one of the best ways to train a steeplechase horse because it allows the horse to jump with other horses and helps build strength and stamina. The similarities in form and function between the two sports is evident in this picture (above) of Hugh O'Donovan, one-time master of the Green Spring Valley Hunt Club, clearing a timber fence in the field; and (below) riders jumping a fence in the Maryland Hunt Cup in the early 1920s.

THE FOUNDERS OF THE MARYLAND HUNT CUP

Mr. Jacob A. Ulman

Mr. Ross W. Whistler

Mr. Frank G. Baldwin

Mr. Gerard T. Hopkins

Mr. Henry J. Farber

In 1894, five gentlemen opted to have a race to determine who had the best jumper in the fox-hunting field. The race that ensued was such a success it became an annual event now known as the Maryland Hunt Cup. The race's founders were Jacob Ulman, Ross Whistler, Frank Baldwin, Gerard Hopkins and Henry Farber. (Courtesy of the Maryland Horse Breeders Association.)

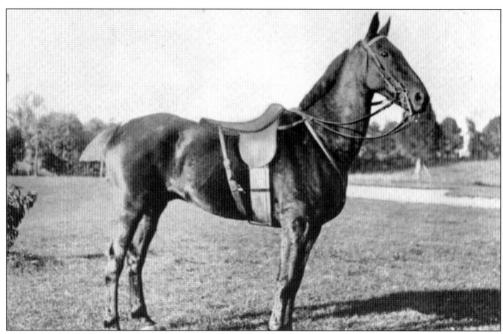

The first Maryland Hunt Cup was won by half a length on May 26, 1894 by Johnny Miller, ridden by his owner John McHenry. There were 12 entries and nine starters at the first race, which was run over a course near what is now the site of St. Paul's School in Brooklandville.

This photo from about 1907 shows Jervis Spencer Jr. up on Garry Owen with the original Green Spring Valley Hunt Club (built in 1897) in the background. The pair won the Maryland Hunt Cup three times in 1901, 1902, and 1907 and won the Grand National in 1902. Jervis Spencer Jr. went on to become the chairman of the Maryland Racing Commission. (Courtesy of Mrs. Hugh O'Donovan.)

This portrait shows Frank A. Bonsal in his hunting attire. He rode in the Maryland Hunt Cup five times, the first in 1899. (Courtesy of Frank Bonsal.)

Princeton, owned by W. J. H. Watters and later by Sidney Watters, was one of the first three-time winners of the Maryland Hunt Cup, securing the silver trophy in 1903, 1905, and 1906. Like the other three-time champion of the era, Garry Owen, Princeton was a Thoroughbred and signaled the move from the half-bred horses ridden when the races began to Thoroughbreds.

Riders, horses and owners still compete for the Maryland Hunt Cup silver tankard and the challenge trophy, which stays with the winner for the year of the win. The owner who wins the race three times can retire the trophy. (Courtesy Douglas Lees.)

The Maryland Hunt Cup in 1915 shows Conqueror in the lead and Talisman close behind. After Ross Whistler introduced the Challenge Cup in 1913, entries in the race rose substantially, because owners wanted to try to win the race three times to retire the cup. In 1915 (the first time the race was run in the Worthington Valley, which would become the race's permanent home in 1922) the race featured an unprecedented 28 entries from four states. Talisman, ridden by Jervis Spencer Jr., won that day in 1915.

Shown here winning the Maryland Hunt Cup is Billy Barton. He was the only horse to ever win the Grand National, the Maryland Hunt Cup (in which he fell at the 19th fence and remounted), and Virginia Gold Cup on consecutive weekends in the same year, 1926. He went on to race in the English Grand National at Aintree. Although he did not win that race, his celebrity status earned him a place on the cover of *Time* magazine in 1929. (Courtesy of Bruce Fenwick.)

Billy Barton's owner, Howard Bruce, and jockey, Albert Ober, are shown here after their Maryland Hunt Cup win in 1926. Before being gelded and turned onto the steeplechase course, Billy Barton had a reputation for being disagreeable on the flat track. (Courtesy of Timothy Naylor.)

Unidentified riders take a fence on the Maryland Hunt Cup course in the 1920s. In 1922, the Maryland Hunt Cup moved to its permanent home in the Worthington Valley.

This photograph shows an early meeting of the My Lady's Manor Race, which had its first start in 1902. After a brief hiatus, the race began again in 1909 and has run ever since. (Courtesy of Timothy Naylor.)

A program from 1926 shows an avid Grand National spectator's race-day notes.

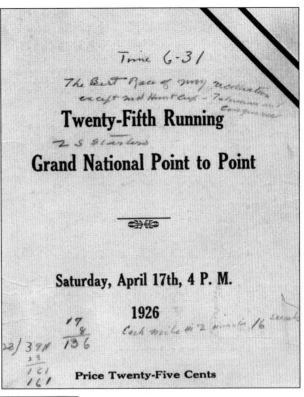

Time 6-31

The Best Race of my recollection except md Hunt Cup - Telemon and Congueror

Twenty-Fifth Running

2 5 Starters

Grand National Point to Point

Saturday, April 17th, 4 P. M.

1926

Each mile #2 minute 16 second

28/ 39# 136
1 7 8
23
1 61
1 6 1

Price Twenty-Five Cents

Joseph Flanagan takes off over a fence in the Maryland Hunt Cup. (Courtesy of Avla Pitts.)

A 1927 photograph shows the start of the Grand National. From 1925 to 1934, the race was run at Brooklandwood, the estate of Capt. Isaac Emerson. Billy Barton won the 1927 race by a slim

margin. (Courtesy of Timothy Naylor.)

Riders at the first fence of the 1929 Grand National include number four, William Street on Reel Foot, and number seven, Frank Bonsal Jr. on Aimwell, who came in first. (Courtesy of Frank Bonsal.)

Frank "Downey" Bonsal is shown on Bon Master in 1934. Bon Master won the My Lady's Manor in 1928 and Maryland Hunt Cup in 1927 and 1928. Bonsal rode in the Maryland Hunt Cup seven times. (Courtesy of Frank Bonsal.)

The 1933 Grand National shows, from left to right, competitors Soleil D'Or and Dr. Ray Woolfe; Mad Boy and Gary Black; Bill Clark and A. G. Ober Jr.; Baby Bunting and John Fenwick; and Brose Hover and Frank "Downey" Bonsal. (Courtesy of The Grand National Committee.)

In perhaps one of the most famous falls of the era, Randy Duffy was unseated from his mount, Fugitive, in the 1933 Maryland Hunt Cup. Shockingly both horse and rider recovered, remounted, and finished fourth. (Courtesy of John Rossell Jr.)

Charles R. White (center) celebrates with his sister, Suzanne Voss Whitman, after his first Maryland Hunt Cup win as the rider of Captain Kettle in 1933. (Courtesy of A. Patrick Smithwick Jr.)

Horses come over the first fence of the "new" Grand National course in 1935. Suburban sprawl forced the race to a site near Hereford, Maryland, where the course of 16 fences ranged over one and a half miles. Nearly 20,000 spectators reportedly turned out to see the event that year. (Courtesy of William Klemm.)

Trouble Maker, ridden by Noel Laing, ekes out a close victory over Brose Hover, ridden by Frank "Downey" Bonsal, in the 1932 Maryland Hunt Cup, setting a new course record. Trouble Maker, who also ran in the English Grand National, died at the 17th fence of the Maryland Hunt Cup in 1935, when he somersaulted over the fence. He was buried where he lay on the course, and stories say his spirit still walks the course. His owner, Marion DuPont Scott, never ran another horse in the Maryland Hunt Cup. (Courtesy of John Rossell Jr.)

Distinguished guests turned out in 1935 at Snow Hill, the estate that is home to the Maryland Hunt Cup. From left to right are Count de Davila, the Romanian minister; Mrs. Henry L. Stimson; Hon. Henry L. Stimson, former secretary of state; Sir Ronald Lindsay, British ambassador; Mrs. John Garrett; Mrs. Tuckerman Draper; Mrs. Henry Leonard, Charles Heiser, and Burrill Hoffman. (Courtesy of Baltimore News.)

In 1935, Latrobe Roosevelt, son of the assistant secretary of the navy, rode in the second race of the My Lady's Manor on Preparedness, owned by Arthur Meigs. (Courtesy of William Klemm.)

The glow of silver dominates this picture of the 1935 cup presentation at the My Lady's Manor. Pictured are Morgan Macy (rider), Mrs. Dean Bedford (donor of the award), and Victor P. Noyes (trainer). (Courtesy of William Klemm.)

John G. Fenwick on Jackanapes and Hugh J. O'Donovan on Justa Racket head to the start of the 1937 My Lady's Manor race. (Courtesy of Charles Fenwick Sr.)

Suzanne Whitman (left), Sterritt Gittings (center), and Frances Warfield are shown here in attendance at the Maryland Hunt Cup. Both young women would go on to marry well-known riders A. P. Smithwick and Regan McKinney, respectively. (Courtesy A. Patrick Smithwick Jr.)

Tailgating and picnicking have long been a part of the race day tradition. (Courtesy of the Library of Congress.)

John K. Shaw leads rider Hugh O'Donovan out of the paddock. Shaw designed the present-day Grand National course of 18 jumps, some as high as four feet and nine inches, situated in Butler, Maryland. The course was first used in 1946 (races were not held during World War II). (Courtesy of Bert Morgan.)

Two

THE THRILL OF COMPETITION

The race was pronounced a most interesting one as the finish was good and horses all fenced superbly, leaving but few broken or injured jumps in the course.

—This report, taken from *The Baltimore Sun* on Sunday, April 19, 1903, tells of the 10th running of the Maryland Hunt Cup in Towson.

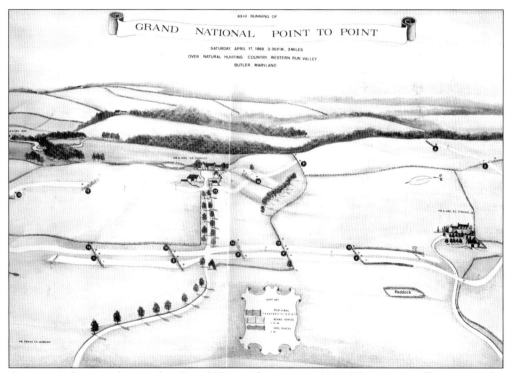

An artist's drawing depicts the Grand National course in 1965. The race is still run over the same course, located in Butler, Maryland.

An aerial photograph of the 1946 My Lady's Manor race shows cars and spectators lining the stretch and the Pearce farm in the background. (Courtesy of Mrs. Carl Shaffer.)

Fred Colwill and Blockade leave all other competitors far behind in a race in 1940. Blockade was an unruly youngster who failed at the track, at attempts to be a show horse, and even at being a foxhunter. But under the direction of trainer Janon Fisher Jr. and rider Fred Colwill, Blockade, a virtual unknown when his dynamic pairing with Fisher began, became a great steeplechase horse. Blockade was the first horse to win the Maryland Hunt Cup three straight times in 1938, 1939, and 1940 (he won the Grand National in 1939), and he set a course record that stood for 22 years with his first win. (Courtesy of Stiles Colwill.)

Stuart Janney Jr., here in the paddock of the Maryland Hunt Cup in 1941, is best known as the owner, rider, and trainer of Winton, who won the My Lady's Manor and Maryland Hunt Cups in 1942, 1946, and 1947 and the Grand National in 1941, 1942, and 1946. His wins in 1942 made him the first horse in history to sweep the entire Big Three of steeplechase racing. When he and Janney retired in 1947, Winton had 12 wins in 13 starts. (Courtesy of Katherine Hoffman.)

After a hiatus for World War II, many returning veterans enjoyed taking the field again, but during the break in racing, a new crop of youngsters was preparing to break onto the scene. Shown from left to right in 1947, Louis Merryman on Roxspur, Worthington Bordley on Clifton's Duke, and Stuart Janney Jr. on Winton come over the 10th fence of the Maryland Hunt Cup. (Courtesy of Bert Morgan.)

Thousands of spectators cram around the snow fencing that delineates the paddock at the 1947 Maryland Hunt Cup, but the horsemen within seem nonplussed by the crowd. They are (from left to right) John Strawbridge, Frank Powers, Benjamin "Laddie" Murray (at Bungtown's head), and Edward Cheston (saddling Bungtown). (Courtesy of Bert Morgan.)

Brothers Walter and Daniel Brewster pose for a quick photograph before the 1949 running of the Maryland Hunt Cup. (Courtesy of Bert Morgan.)

The horses jumping the first fence of the Maryland Hunt Cup in either 1949 or 1950 include Tiger Bennett, Grover Stephens on Count Stefan, Jay Secor on Bomber, and D. M. "Mikey" Smithwick on Pine Pep. (Courtesy of Bert Morgan.)

Mikey Smithwick brings Pine Pep over the Maryland Hunt Cup course in 1950. Pine Pep (owned by Mrs. W. J. Clothier and trained by Burling Cocks) and Smithwick dominated the steeplechase scene in Maryland in the late 1940s and early 1950s. Pine Pep secured multiple wins in every Big Three race and even went to Aintree in England, although he failed to qualify and retired shortly thereafter. (Courtesy of Bert Morgan.)

Bomber, aptly named and held by an unidentified man, fell at the 11th fence of the 1951 Maryland Hunt Cup, bringing down with him the race-day favorite, Pine Pep ridden by Mikey Smithwick, losing them their shot at what may have been a third straight win. (Courtesy of D. M. Smithwick.)

The 1951 Maryland Hunt Cup race, shown here, was marred by accident and injury starting at the third fence, where three horses fell, and two were fatally injured. Four more horses would fall that day, and one would be forced out of bounds when a patrol judge rode onto the course. Jester's Moon reigned victorious at the end. (Courtesy of Bert Morgan.)

Not all racing is glory, as seen in this photograph of a rider falling in the 1953 Maryland Hunt Cup. (Courtesy of the News-Post American.)

The finish of the 1955 John Rush Streett Memorial was a close one, as Dr. J. M. Rogers on Star Salone and Frank A. Bonsal Jr. on Borobash (the eventual winner) battle to the end in front of a reported crowd of 6,000. The race is run on the same day as the My Lady's Manor and is for horses that have never won two races over timber. (Courtesy of Frank Bonsal.)

Land's Corner, ridden by Benjamin H. "Laddie" Murray, secures a wide margin of victory in the 1955 Maryland Hunt Cup. (Courtesy of Bert Morgan.)

In 1956, Grover Stephens and Infraction fell at the 13th fence of the Maryland Hunt Cup. (Courtesy of Fred Thomas.)

Mikey Smithwick continued to solidify his position as the don of steeplechase racing with his Maryland Hunt Cup win on Fluctuate in 1960. The pair is led by Herb Madden. (Courtesy of D.M. Smithwick.)

Jack Griswold on Doll Ram and Benjamin H. "Laddie" Murray on Mainstay take the 12th fence of the Maryland Hunt Cup in 1960. Doll Ram would later fall at the 14th, and Mainstay finished second. (Courtesy of Bert Morgan.)

Benjamin H. "Laddie" Murray on Flying Cub (left) and James "Jamie" Hruska on Go Bid Go make a beautiful pair, competing closely in the 1961 Grand National. (Courtesy of Mr. and Mrs. C. N. Bliss III.)

The moment every rider and owner anticipates is the cup presentation. Here Frances Cochran Smith, Cornelius Bliss (owner), and James Hruska celebrate Go Bid Go's 1961 Grand National win. (Courtesy of Mr. and Mrs. C. N. Bliss III.)

J. W. Y. Martin jumps with Beachcomber (left) in the 1963 Grand National. (Courtesy of Peter Winants.)

Although difficult to make out, horses in the 1963 Grand National are coming over the course's water jump. (Courtesy of Peter Winants.)

A close field of riders press over a fence in the Grand National in the 1960s, while one rider loses his seat. (Courtesy of Baltimore News-Post American.)

The rolling landscape in Butler, Maryland, which has played host to the Grand National since 1946, is ideal for steeplechasing. The area has changed little since this photograph was taken in 1966. (Courtesy of the Maryland Horse Breeders Association.)

Janon Fisher III saddles up Mountain Dew for the 1963 Grand National, which he would win. Fisher and Mountain Dew dominated the Grand National throughout the 1960s (they won the race six times), and they won the Maryland Hunt Cup in 1962, 1965, and 1967. Mountain Dew was trained by Fisher's father, Janon Fisher Jr., who also trained the famous Blockade. (Courtesy of Frank Bonsal.)

The story of Crompton "Tommy" Smith Jr. and horse Jay Trump, shown here with Herb Madden at the Maryland Hunt Cup, began at the Charles Town racetrack, where Smith picked up the poorly performing horse with the badly scarred knee. Despite his humble beginnings, Jay Trump flourished under the tutelage of two great trainers, H. Robertson Fenwick and D. M. Smithwick, and his rider, Smith. After sweeping the Big Three races in 1964, the pair went to England, where Jay Trump became the only American bred, owned, and ridden horse to win the English Grand National. Their story became a book, *The Will to Win*, and the stuff of steeplechase legend. (Courtesy of Peter Winants.)

Janon Fisher III on Mountain Dew and Crompton "Tommy" Smith Jr. on Jay Trump battle for the win in the 1966 Grand National. The rivalry between Mountain Dew and Jay Trump was one of the greatest in steeplechase history, lasting almost a decade. One fellow rider remembers

a Maryland Hunt Cup run in the fog in the 1960s when all that could be heard in the misty quiet was the stirrups of Mountain Dew and Jay Trump banging together as the two horses went stride for stride. (Courtesy of Peter Winants.)

Horses jump the ninth fence in the Grand National in 1966. The race was won by Janon Fisher III on Mountain Dew. (Courtesy of Peter Winants.)

Janon Fisher III (left) enjoys his fifth time on the winner's stand at the Grand National in 1967. Also pictured from left to right are Frances Cochran, Mrs. Fisher (Janon III's mother and Janon Jr.'s wife), Janon Fisher Jr., and unidentified. (Courtesy of Peter Winants.)

Horses and riders approach a fence at the Grand National course in 1968 in the Benjamin H. Murray Memorial race. The race was initiated on Grand National day in 1966 and is named for Benjamin H. "Laddie" Murray, the avid steeplechase rider. The race is for horses five years old or older who have not won two races over timber at a recognized meeting. (Courtesy of Peter Winants.)

Mountain Dew and Janon Fisher III try for a fourth win in the Maryland Hunt Cup in 1968 but would later pull up, quitting the race because Mountain Dew bowed a tendon; patrol judge Jervis Finney looks on. Having ridden the Maryland Hunt Cup eight times, winning it three, *American Steeplechasing* reported that a rail from the course was buried with Mountain Dew when he died in 1979. (Courtesy of Peter Winants.)

Louis "Paddy" Neilson III takes the stand for his win on Sea Master at the 1965 My Lady's Manor. Neilson would become familiar with the view from the stand in a career that spanned five decades. From left to right are Polly Riggs, Redmond Stewart, Barbara Obre, Louis Neilson, Nina Nielson, and unidentified. (Courtesy of Peter Winants.)

Because the Maryland Hunt Cup course is divided by Tufton Road in the Worthington Valley, the pavement is covered with dirt and mulch to allow riders to gallop across the hard surface, as can be seen in this photograph from 1968. (Courtesy of Peter Winants.)

In 1968, the John Rush Streett Memorial went to Conasauga. Pictured are owner Frank Bonsal, Helen Bonsal, the Fisher family, and the winning rider, Louis Neilson III. (Courtesy of the Maryland Horse Breeders Association.)

Horses thunder toward the finish in the Grand National in 1968, the last year it was won by Mountain Dew. (Courtesy of Peter Winants.)

Dr. John R. S. Fisher finished first in the 1969 Maryland Hunt Cup on his own horse, Landing Party, on whom he also swept the Grand National in the years between 1969 and 1971 (although the rider in 1969 was Louis Neilson III). Dr. Fisher's son would carry on the tradition of racing in the family. (Courtesy of Mrs. Hugh O'Donovan.)

Riders approach a plank fence in the 1970 renewal of the My Lady's Manor, which was won by owner/rider Dr. John R. S. Fisher on Landing Party. (Courtesy of Peter Winants.)

Spectators climb onto the roofs of cars or press against snow fencing to watch the 10th jump of the My Lady's Manor. (Courtesy of the Maryland Horse Breeders Association.)

Dr. John R. S. Fisher enjoys a strong lead on Landing Party at the finish of the 1971 Maryland Hunt Cup. (Courtesy of Peter Winants.)

Riders and horses meet in the paddock of the old My Lady's Manor course—run over the property of the Secors and Pearces—where spectators can enjoy their first peek at the day's competitors. (Courtesy of the Maryland Horse Breeders Association.)

After saddling up, riders leave the paddock for the start of the My Lady's Manor. (Courtesy of Peter Winants.)

Much-to-Do, ridden by owner/rider J. B. Secor, clears a fence at the old course of the My Lady's Manor, which was run over property owned by his family (as well as portions of the Pearce, Riggs, and Warfield family farms) until 1978. (Courtesy of Peter Winants.)

The second-to-last fence of the 1972 Grand National proved unlucky for Frank Bonsal, who fell off Conasauga as J. W. Y. "Duck" Martin clears off on Early Earner. (Courtesy of Frank Bonsal.)

Spectators are able to get up close and personal with the race day action as can be seen in the picture of the 13th fence of the Maryland Hunt Cup with Evening Mail, Early Earner, and Morning Mac in 1973. (Courtesy of Douglas Lees.)

At the 1973 renewal of the Benjamin H. Murray Memorial, Jack Griswold, riding Handsome Daddy, tries to gain on Frank Chapot riding Evening Mail. (Courtesy of Douglas Lees.)

A lost rider does not diminish the competitive spirit of Mod Man, who continued to race in the My Lady's Manor in 1980 despite losing rider Toinette Jackson at the fifth fence.

(Courtesy of Douglass Lees.)

Riders in colorful silks prepare for the 1975 Maryland Hunt Cup. Russell Jones Jr. on Jacko, wearing the blue silks with the yellow cross of Shiloh Farm, would go on to win. Turney McKnight is in the background on Hammurabi. (Courtesy of Douglas Lees.)

Although R. Penn Smith "Buzz" Hannum is secure in the lead of the 1976 running of the Grand National, Charles Fenwick Jr. on Mimaccia is not so lucky, as he busts out the rail. (Courtesy of Douglas Lees.)

In 1977, H. Turney McKnight, owner and rider, set a new course record at the My Lady's Manor with his win on Matlow. McKnight retired the Challenge Cup with his record-setting third win at the old Manor course. McKnight is now the director of the My Lady's Manor race. (Courtesy of H. T. McKnight.)

Don Yovanovich and Count Turk enjoy a straight ride over the ninth fence and on to the winner's circle at the 1977 Benjamin H. Murray Memorial race. (Courtesy of Douglas Lees.)

Charles C. Fenwick Jr. on Ben Nevis II at the 1976 Grand National is shown here. Fenwick was raised on a farm adjacent to the Maryland Hunt Cup course and grew up aspiring to win the coveted tankard. After exhaustive training to calm the high-strung horse owned by renowned horseman Redmond C. Stewart Jr., Fenwick and Ben Nevis II began sweeping races, from the maiden race at the My Lady's Manor to course records at the Grand National and Maryland Hunt Cup. In 1980, Fenwick and Ben Nevis II enjoyed a historic win at the English Grand National, capturing the glory that eluded Fenwick's grandfather, who owned Billy Barton when he went to Aintree and lost in 1928. (Courtesy of Douglas Lees.)

Horses parade through the paddock at the My Lady's Manor new course, set parallel to Jarrettsville Pike near the Elkridge Harford Hunt Club in 1978. (Courtesy of Douglas Lees.)

Many horses and riders prepare for the Big Three races by participating in the Elkridge Harford Point-to-Point shown here with H. Turney McKnight and Tong jumping the last fence of the maiden timber race in 1979. While not a National Steeplechase Association-sanctioned race, it is a good training and proving ground for what is to come in the spring races. (Courtesy of Douglas Lees.)

In 1979, Toinette Jackson Neilson, pictured with Jane Bassett, became the first woman to win the My Lady's Manor with her victory on Mod Man. (Courtesy of Douglas Lees.)

D. M. "Speedy" Smithwick Jr., son of the well-known rider and trainer Mikey Smithwick, jumps the 13th fence of the Maryland Hunt Cup on Moon Meeting in his first ride around the course. (Courtesy of Douglas Lees.)

When the Maryland Hunt Cup was won by a woman jockey for the first time in 1980, the win was a family affair that placed three generations of women onto the winners stand and in the history books. The winning horse, Cancottage, was owned by Mrs. Miles Valentine (left), ridden by her granddaughter Joy Slater (in the Valentines' signature silks), and trained by Jill Fanning, Mrs. Valentine's daughter. (Courtesy of Douglas Lees.)

It's a difficult day for Seek and Destroy, who lost rider Nick Schweizer at the last fence of the Benjamin H. Murray memorial race in 1989. The winner, Cabral, won by 15 lengths. (Courtesy of Nina Ewing.)

Elizabeth McKnight had a challenging ride to finish first in the 1986 Maryland Hunt Cup. She and Tong not only jumped the third fence, but Broderick Munroe-Wilson as well after he fell on Guinea Man. (Courtesy of Nina Ewing.)

Elizabeth McKnight won the Maryland Hunt Cup in 1986 on Tong. In 1982, husband H. Turney McKnight also won the race on Tong, making the couple the only husband-and-wife duo to win the Maryland Hunt Cup. (Courtesy of Douglas Lees.)

Sometimes it's nice to go it alone, like John Coles (rider and trainer) and Appolinax, who are shown here at the eighth fence of the My Lady's Manor. They came in first in the 1985 race. (Courtesy of Douglas Lees.)

It was a close call at the finish when Charles C. Fenwick Jr. (left) secured his fifth win of the Maryland Hunt Cup in 1987 on Sugar Bee over John Hannum (right) on Our Climber. (Courtesy of Douglas Lees.)

Two generations of riders battle to the finish line spattered in mud at the 1989 Maryland Hunt Cup. At left is the veteran Louis "Paddy" Neilson III on Uncle Merlin, enjoying his 16th ride in the race at age 47. At his right is the youthful William Meister, who regained his position at the front despite falling off at the first fence. But it was not enough. The win went to Neilson that day. (Courtesy of Douglas Lees.)

Irvin Naylor shows perfect form on Probon, whose hoof is nicely folded at the elbow as he soars well over the 10th fence of the Maryland Hunt Cup in 1988. (Courtesy of Irvin S. Naylor.)

In 1991, Blythe Miller joined the ranks of women making history in steeplechase racing when she became the first woman to win the Grand National. (Courtesy of Nina Ewing.)

Like his brother, Charles C. Fenwick Jr., Bruce Fenwick shares a familial love of steeplechase racing. Here he can be seen in 1990 winning his first Grand National on Big Conoy with William Meister trailing behind on The Hard Word. (Courtesy of Douglas Lees.)

In 1992, Patrick Worrall and Von Csadek won the Maryland Hunt Cup, capping off a long ride to victory. The pair had already won the Virginia Gold Cup by the greatest margin in the race's history when Worrall was just 16 years old. In 1988, Von Csadek was named Horse of the Year. Despite wins in the My Lady's Manor, the Maryland Hunt Cup was elusive. In 1989, they fell at the 14th fence. In 1990, Worrall was unseated at the water jump, losing a tremendous lead. Finally, in 1992, Worrall obtained victory by 100 lengths on the day of his mother's birthday. (Courtesy of Douglas Lees.)

A close field of competitors—Sortou, Sarkis, Welter Weight, Gus's Boy, and Ivory Poacher—jumps the 14th fence of the My Lady's Manor. Ivory Poacher, ridden by Sanna Neilson, would come from behind to finish first. (Courtesy of Douglas Lees.)

Irvin S. Naylor won the Benjamin H. Murray Memorial in 1996 on Emerald Action. Like many steeplechase enthusiasts, Naylor began his career as a youngster, riding in his first Maryland Hunt Cup race in 1953 when he was just a junior in high school. (Courtesy of Douglas Lees.)

In 1995, Anne Moran won the Maryland Hunt Cup on Buck Jakes, one of the best timber horses of the 1990s, seen with Peyton Cochran and trainer Charles C. Fenwick Jr. Buck Jakes's Irish-born rider was a young mother at the time, and his trainer was a champion rider himself. Under their watchful eyes, Buck Jakes won the Grand National in 1994, 1997, and 1998 and the Maryland Hunt Cup again in 1997. The Hunt Cup win in 1995 ironically broke the course record that was set by Buck Jakes's trainer, Charles Fenwick Jr., on Ben Nevis II. (Courtesy of Douglas Lees.)

It was a fight to the finish in the 1998 Maryland Hunt Cup between Michael Elmore on Welter Weight and Joseph G. Davies on Florida Law, . . .

. . . but it was Florida Law who took home the victory. (Courtesy of Joseph G. Davies.)

The year for Solo Lord was 2001, shown here after winning the Maryland Hunt Cup with his rider, Michael Hoffman, Regina Welsh (an assistant to trainer Bruce Miller), and Joe Cassidy. (Courtesy of Douglas Lees.)

Throughout the years, the equipment has changed from silk skull caps to elaborate riding hats, protective vests, and goggles, but the thrill of a close finish remains the same, as seen in this close finish from the My Lady's Manor. (Courtesy of Douglas Lees.)

Jack Ball walks Florida Law through a race paddock. (Courtesy of Douglas Lees.)

Iron Fist, ridden by Roger Horgan, races to the finish in the My Lady's Manor. The horse, owned by John H. Filbert III, dominated the Manor race for three years starting in 2000.

When the Grand National was begun in 1898 by a handful of bold teenagers, it was a race for boys age 15 and under on ponies. Although the race grew up with the boys and is now for adult riders on horses, there are still pony races at the Grand National each year, inspiring a new generation of steeplechase riders. (Courtesy of Douglas Lees.)

Charles C. Fenwick III (left) continued a family tradition with his first Big Three win at the My Lady's Manor in 2004 on Askim. Also pictured are Blair Waterman (center) on Sam Sullivan and Michelle Hunter on Joe At Six. (Courtesy of Douglas Lees.)

Three

THE CULTURE OF
THE HORSE

*Marion Miller and Grace Smith of Buffalo are coming down for both the Grand National
Saturday and the Maryland Hunt Cup. It's really surprising sometimes how many people
from out of town come down here just for these steeplechases!*

—"Gossip of the Week," *The Baltimore Sun*, April 17, 1932.

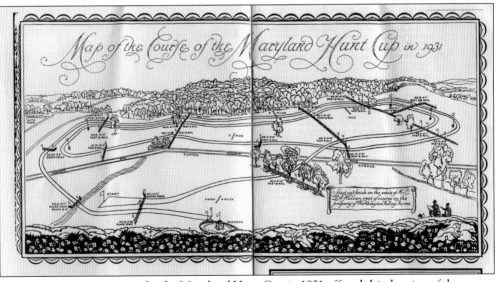

A commemorative program for the Maryland Hunt Cup in 1931 offered this drawing of the course
in the Worthington Valley. The course remains as it was then: 22 jumps over approximately four
miles of open terrain.

In the 1920s, a crowd gathers around Snow Hill, the estate that tops the hill overlooking the Maryland Hunt Cup course. (Courtesy of Timothy Naylor.)

Spectators crush around the Maryland Hunt Cup paddock in 1926, while cars line the finish line in the distance. (Courtesy of Timothy Naylor.)

After Billy Barton's big win at the Maryland Hunt Cup, spectators swarmed owner Howard Bruce (looking at the camera at left) and rider Albert Ober (in the white jockey's cap). (Courtesy of Timothy Naylor.)

A Maryland Hunt Cup race attendee inspects a directional sign indicating the way to local farms. The sign was reportedly erected by the owner of John Brown's General Store when he grew weary of people always stopping in his store for directions. (Courtesy of the Maryland Horse Breeders Association)

Mrs. Redmond C. Stewart (Katherine), wife of the well-known horseman who rode in the first Maryland Hunt Cups, is flanked by spectators at the 1924 running of the Grand National at Five Farms. (Courtesy of Timothy Naylor.)

Mikey Smithwick and Mrs. W. J. Clothier, rider and owner of Pine Pep respectively, have a casual chat before the 1949 Maryland Hunt Cup. Smithwick and Pine Pep won that year, and the next, and in 1952. (Courtesy of D. M. Smithwick.)

It could be said that J. Fred Colwill and his wife, Marion Tuttle, were brought together by a horse. After Colwill won the Maryland Hunt Cup for the third time in 1940 on the renowned Blockade, his owner, Mrs. E. Read Beard, sold the horse to Charles E. Tuttle. One year later, Colwill married Tuttle's daughter, Marion, and continued to ride Blockade under his new ownership. (Courtesy of Stiles Colwill.)

Mr. and Mrs. Redmond C. Stewart Jr. make a fine portrait in their hunting attire. (Courtesy of Beth Fenwick.)

Race day attire was—and sometimes still is—a dressy affair, as evidenced by Betty Wickes-Nichols and an unidentified man. The clothing of race goers was frequently commented on in the gossip columns of the local newspapers. (Courtesy of Mrs. Hugh O'Donovan.)

J. W. S. "Monk" Foster and an unidentified guest arrive in style at the Maryland Hunt Cup. (Courtesy of John Foster.)

Frank Bonsal III poses with his father Frank "Downey" Bonsal Jr. after his win at the Maryland Hunt Cup on Lancrel in 1956. Between the two men, they ran the race ten times and represent generations of steeplechase racing. (Courtesy of Frank Bonsal.)

Gill Fenwick, pictured here in 1953, was instrumental in helping to train Jay Trump and many other steeplechase success stories along with husband H. Robertson Fenwick. (Courtesy of Carol Fenwick.)

Joseph France and Mary Riker enjoy a picnic spread. (Courtesy of D. M. Smithwick.)

The hillside at Snow Hill fills with spectators for the Maryland Hunt Cup in the 1960s. (Courtesy of Peter Winants.)

Some days, umbrellas as colorful as jockey's silks are more plentiful on the racecourse than picnics. (Courtesy of Maryanna Skowronski.)

A little rain does not dampen the spirit of picnickers, riders, or spectators at the My Lady's Manor course. (Courtesy of Cappy Jackson.)

Elaborate tailgates, such as this one at the My Lady's Manor, are an integral part of the full race-day experience. (Courtesy of Cappy Jackson.)

The races attract many dedicated followers. Robert M. Six was an outrider—responsible for keeping the course clear of people and loose horses—the last year the My Lady's Manor ran at the old course. Now in his 90s, he has only missed the My Lady's Manor a handful of times in his lifetime. (Courtesy of Maryanna Skowronski.)

Clinton Pitts (left), George Clement (center), and Cornelius Bliss would be a familiar sight at any race. All were masters of fox hounds of the Elkridge Harford Hunt Club, and Bliss owned the steeplechase horse Go Bid Go. (Courtesy of Mr. and Mrs. C. N. Bliss III.)

It's not uncommon to see a steeplechase competitor out in the hunting field. Here Gill Fenwick (left), Acsah O'Donovan (center), and Catherine Allan depart for a day of hunting, each on a timber-winning horse. (Courtesy of Mrs. Hugh O'Donovan.)

Charles C. Fenwick Jr., Mary Lawrason Wing, and Frank Bonsal are pictured here from left to right at the first awarding of the Bryce Wing Memorial Trophy in 1980. The award, which is given annually to the person who does the most for timber racing in Maryland, went to Fenwick in 1980, the same year he won the English Grand National. (Courtesy of the Maryland Horse Breeders Association.)

John Bosley IV and Mrs. E. J. Todd are shown here after Bosley rode Mrs. Todd's horse, Art Dom, to victory in the B. Frank Christmas Memorial race, a precursor to the Big Three races. Like many other riders, horses were a family affair for Bosley, whose father and grandfather were horsemen. His grandmother was also a trainer. (Courtesy of Douglas Lees.)

Elizabeth "Betty" Bird trained two Maryland Hunt Cup winners, Marchized and Fort Devon. (Courtesy of Douglas Lees.)

Professional and amateur photographers alike vie for precarious positions to get the best shot on race day. Here they are photographing the 13th fence of the 1970 Maryland Hunt Cup. (Courtesy of Peter Winants.)

For several years, bagpipers entertained race goers at the My Lady's Manor. (Courtesy of Douglas Lees.)

Louis "Paddy" Neilson III has had an astonishingly long and successful career as a jockey in timber racing. He won the Grand National five times in five straight decades (1958, 1969, 1974, 1986, and 1995) and has ridden in the Maryland Hunt Cup 21 times, the most ever, winning it three times (1968, 1974, and 1989). (Courtesy of Douglas Lees.)

Over the years, some races have evolved and modernized. Corporate-sponsored tents lining the finish line at the My Lady's Manor in 2000 are now a common occurrence. (Courtesy of H. Turney McKnight.)

Spectators at the Maryland Hunt Cup standing at the third fence of the race give an indication of its height. The Big Three are timber races, races over post-and-rail or post-and-board fences that, unlike a brush fence, are solid and unforgiving. One of the fences is referred to as the "Union Memorial," for the local hospital where many riders end up after a fall. (Courtesy of Joseph G. Davies.)

An overhead shot of the parking lot of the Maryland Hunt Cup takes in the tailgating scene in the 1970s. (Courtesy of Douglas Lees.)

Margaret and Walter Brewster prepare to attend the Hunt Ball, which takes place every year on the night of the Maryland Hunt Cup. The event is one of the last white-tie formal events still in existence in the area. (Courtesy of Walter Brewster.)

Two generations of horsemen, C. J. Meister and son William Meister, enjoy a laugh in the paddock of the Grand National. (Courtesy of Douglas Lees.)

Dr. John R. S. Fisher was a common name on the winner's stand in the early 1970s, racking up wins in the My Lady's Manor in 1970, the Grand National in 1970 and 1971, and the Maryland Hunt Cup in 1969 and 1971. (Courtesy of Douglas Lees.)

Falls are an inevitable, if unsettling, part of steeplechasing. Charles C. Fenwick Jr. was unhurt when he was unseated from Happy Orphan in the 1974 Maryland Hunt Cup. (Courtesy of Douglas Lees.)

In the mid-1970s, J.B. Secor (left) and Tom Voss were riders and friends; now both train horses. (Courtesy of Douglas Lees.)

Cary Jackson, owner of Moon Meeting and a former master of the Green Spring Valley Hounds, creates a debonair picture overlooking a paddock area. (Courtesy of Douglas Lees.)

Riders Charles C. Fenwick Jr., Alicia Murphy, and Joe G. Davies get some time to relax in the paddock before race time at the Grand National. (Courtesy of the Maryland Horse Breeders Association.)

Charlie "Sprat" Reeves is a jovial
fixture at all the races in recent years.
(Courtesy of Douglas Lees.)

Sybil Dukehart opts against a car, choosing to arrive at the My Lady's Manor race in old-fashioned style in a horse and carriage. (Courtesy of Nina Ewing.)

Not all race days are picture perfect. Thankfully when the rain pours down (as it did in this photograph from 1989), there's always a tractor nearby to help rescue stuck spectators. (Courtesy of Cappy Jackson.)

Bruce Miller carries tack in 1994. Miller is an owner and trainer as well as the father of champion jockeys Blythe and Chip Miller. (Courtesy of Douglas Lees.)

Mimi Voss holds tight to the trophy earned after Sam Sullivan's win at the 100th running of the Grand National in 2002. (Courtesy of Douglas Lees.)

Iron Fist, with Roger Horgan up, is led by M. J. Kirwin at the My Lady's Manor, a race the pair won three straight times from 2000 to 2002. (Courtesy of Douglas Lees.)

A shot of horses making a turn on the My Lady's Manor course shows just how close spectators come to the race-day action. (Courtesy of H. Turney McKnight.)

Since 1984, the My Lady's Manor race has been run to benefit The Ladew Topiary Gardens, which are adjacent to the racecourse outside of Jarrettsville. The world-famous gardens attract many visitors, but none so unique as these, when in 1979, the Elkridge Harford Hunt Club rode through. They are pictured riding through a topiary rendition of a hunt scene; the hounds in the foreground are topiary.

In 1991, the wonders of video replay technology attracted the attention of many spectators at the Grand National. (Courtesy of Nina Ewing.)

The Wild Goose Chase took place in 1998. The flat race was open to jockeys who rode the Grand National prior to 1990. It was won by Irvin Naylor, then age 62, on Tarsky. Pictured are, from left to right, (first row) Liz McKnight, Crompton "Tommy" Smith, Duncan Patterson, Janon Fisher, and Ben Griswold III; (second row) Jay Griswold, Carl "Bunny" Meister, Irvin Naylor, Turney McKnight, Russell Jones, Tom Voss, and Douglas Worrall. (Courtesy of Douglas Lees.)

Arthur W. Arundel owned Sugar Bee, who won the Maryland Hunt Cup in 1987. His involvement in the sport includes being on the board of directors of the National Steeplechase Association and chairman of the Virginia Gold Cup. (Courtesy of Douglas Lees.)

Dolly Fisher, owner of Matchless, is shown here after his win of the Murray Memorial in 2001 . She was also the owner of Revelstoke, who won the centennial running of the Maryland Hunt Cup and was ridden by her son, Jack. (Courtesy of Douglas Lees.)

Winners of the Junior Hunt Cup accept their prizes in April 2001. The race was begun to encourage young riders to explore the sport of steeplechase riding. Young riders compete based on age and ability wearing real jockey silks. It is unusual for children to wear adult jockey gear, and it is a big deal for the ones who are competing. (Courtesy of Maryanna Skowronski.)

It was a rain-sodden, muddy win for Joe G. Davies and Make-Me-A-Champ in the 2005 running of the Maryland Hunt Cup. Blair Waterman on Bug River placed a close second. (Courtesy of Douglas Lees.)

Four

YESTERDAY AND TODAY

Picnickers enjoyed the sunshine while small fry—and there were many—picked bunches of grape hyacinths growing in purple streaks near the judges stand.

—Reporting on the Grand National, *The Baltimore American*, April 22, 1962.

Mrs. J. W. Clothier's well-known steeplechase horse from the 1950s, Pine Pep, is depicted in paint and surrounded by his four Maryland Hunt Cup winning tankards. (Courtesy of Peter Winants.)

In 1968, Kathy Kusner, shown here weighing in before a race, opened the world of steeplechase racing to women when she petitioned the Maryland Racing Commission for a jockey's license. In 1971, the one-time Olympic rider made history as the first woman to ride in the Maryland Hunt Cup, finishing sixth on Whackerjack. (Courtesy of Peter Winants.)

Since Kathy Kusner's time, women have made successful inroads into all the Big Three races and steeplechase riding in general. Blair Waterman, shown at the Benjamin H. Murray Memorial race, is currently a leading amateur jockey. (Courtesy of Douglas Lees.)

Spectators cram around the finish line and fill the hillside overlooking the Maryland Hunt Cup course in the 1920s.

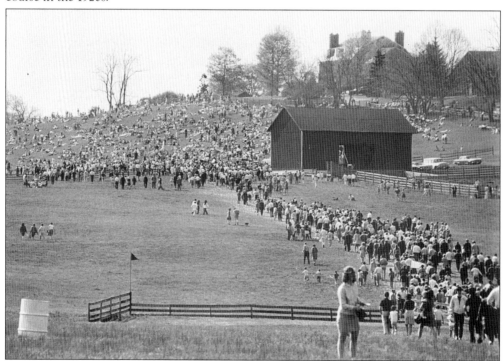

The hillside remains the best vantage point from which to view the Maryland Hunt Cup. Here, spectators stream onto the course from the general parking lot. (Courtesy of Peter Winants.)

A. P. "Paddy" Smithwick (left), age 10, and D. M. "Mikey" Smithwick, age 8, shown on their ponies Jazz and Napoleon, began their riding careers young. (Courtesy of A. Patrick Smithwick Jr.)

As adults, the Smithwick brothers made names for themselves, Paddy as a jockey and Mikey as a trainer (despite his earlier career as a jockey in which he repeatedly won in all the Big Three contests, including the Maryland Hunt Cup an unprecedented six times). Both are now in the Hall of Fame at the National Museum of Racing in New York. (Courtesy of A. Patrick Smithwick Jr.)

Although he started in the first Maryland Hunt Cup, Redmond C. Stewart would not win until 1904, when he won on Landslide, pictured here. In that race, he beat his brother, racing on The Squire, and was the only horse to finish. (Courtesy of Timothy Naylor.)

Redmond C. Stewart Jr. continued the long tradition of his family in steeplechasing. He rode in the Maryland Hunt Cup six times and owned the famous Ben Nevis II. Like his father, he is regarded as one of the preeminent horsemen of his time. Now his daughter, Ann, continues that tradition as a trainer. (Courtesy of Douglas Lees.)

In 1982, the viewing stand atop the hill at the My Lady's Manor was little more than a rickety assembly of scaffolding. (Courtesy of H. Turney McKnight.)

Now the race has a permanent wooden viewing stand complete with audio/visual technology. (Courtesy of H. Turney McKnight.)

A snapshot of the 1955 Maryland Hunt Cup presentation shows, from left to right, Mr. and Mrs. William Strawbridge (owners), Benjamin H. Murray (rider), Barbara West (trainer), and Edward M. Cheston (trainer) the year Land's Corner won. Land's Corner was awarded status as the nation's outstanding timber horse in 1954, the same year he set the course record at the My Lady's Manor. (Courtesy of Bert Morgan.)

Edward Murray (with binoculars) presents the trophy for the race named for his brother, The Benjamin H. Murray Memorial, which is run on the same day as the Grand National. The race was founded in 1966. Also pictured are Neil Morris, Gov. Robert L. Erhlich, and the governor's father. (Courtesy of Edward Murray.)

The Maryland Hunt Cup course has not changed since it settled in its permanent place in 1922, and neither has the allure of picnicking on the hillside overlooking the course. (Courtesy of Timothy Naylor.)

Although the only cars allowed on the course now are race vehicles, there is still nothing better than watching the race from the hillside with a full picnic hamper nearby. (Courtesy of Peter Winants.)

Fred Colwill and an unidentified horse make a dramatic leap over a fence in the My Lady's Manor in the late 1930s. (Courtesy of Mrs. Hugh O'Donovan.)

Competition is just as aggressive today, as evidenced by Roger Horgan, William Meister, and Joe G. Davies in the 2000 running of the My Lady's Manor. (Courtesy of Douglas Lees.)

In 1968, A. Patrick Smithwick Jr. on Moonlore won his first major race, the Benjamin H. Murray Memorial. He was just a junior in high school. A. Patrick Smithwick Jr. is Paddy Smithwick's son. (Courtesy of Peter Winants.)

Years after his first go around the Grand National course, A. Patrick Smithwick returned in 2001 to win on Welter Weight. His uncle, Mikey Smithwick, was there to congratulate the winner. The horse was accustom to praise, having already won the race in 1999 and 2000. (Courtesy of D. M. Smithwick.)

Benjamin Griswold III is flanked by his sons Benjamin Griswold IV and Jay Griswold in the hunting field. (Courtesy B. H. Griswold IV.)

Jay Griswold is shown here before a race. Despite running in the Maryland Hunt Cup 17 times, he never secured a win, but the Griswold name remains synonymous with steeplechase racing. (Courtesy of Douglas Lees.)

Louis "Paddy" Neilson III is shown on the winner's stand with his young daughters in the early 1970s. (Courtesy of the Maryland Horse Breeders Association.)

Neilson's daughter Sanna Neilson Hendricks, shown in 1994, is now an accomplished rider in her own right who has twice won both the My Lady's Manor and Maryland Hunt Cup. (Courtesy of Nina Ewing.)

In 1987, Charles C. Fenwick III helps his father, Charles C. Fenwick Jr., prepare his tack on race day. (Courtesy of Douglas Lees.)

In 2003, Charles C. Fenwick III shares his Benjamin H. Murray Memorial win with his daughter, Annie. Also pictured are Jack Shaw, Ann Stewart, Emily Fenwick, and Margaret Fenwick. (Courtesy of Douglas Lees.)

Jack Fisher and brother Rush make off with the Maryland Hunt cup trophy after their father's win on Landing Party. (Courtesy of Douglas Lees.)

In 1994, it was Jack Fisher who earned the trophy when he captured the Maryland Hunt Cup on Revelstoke. Pictured from left to right are John R. S. Fisher, Jack Fisher, Dolly Fisher, Polly Riggs, and Mrs. J. W. Y. Martin. (Courtesy of Douglas Lees.)